WITHDRAWN

The Countries

Israel

WITHDRAWN

Bob Italia , 1955 -

ABDO Publishing Company

visit us at
www.abdopub.com

Published by ABDO Publishing Company, 4940 Viking Drive, Edina, Minnesota 55435.
Copyright © 2001 by Abdo Consulting Group, Inc. International copyrights reserved in
all countries. No part of this book may be reproduced in any form without written
permission from the publisher.

Printed in the United States.

Photos: Corbis, AP/Wide World
Editors: Tamara L. Britton and Kate A. Furlong
Art Direction & Maps: Neil Klinepier

Library of Congress Cataloging-in-Publication Data

Italia, Bob, 1955-
   Israel / Bob Italia.
     p. cm. -- (The countries)
   Includes index.
   ISBN 1-57765-497-8
    1. Israel--Juvenile literature. [1. Israel.] I. Title. II. Series.

DS102.95 .I92 2001
956.94--dc21

                                                 2001016126

Contents

Shalom!

Greetings from Israel! Israel is a modern country with ancient roots. It is the historical and spiritual homeland of the Jewish people. Over time, other groups have settled there, too.

Israel is a small country, but it has many types of land. Mountains, lakes, deserts, plains, and coastlines are all part of Israel's geography. This varied landscape provides homes for many plants and animals.

The majority of Israel's people live in cities. Some have service jobs or work in factories. Others live in the country and work on farms. The hard work of the Israeli people has helped the country's **economy** grow.

Today, Israel faces many challenges. Some groups in the Middle East want to overtake Israel's land. Despite this, Israelis have built a strong nation that is unlike any other on earth.

Shalom *from Israel!*

Fast Facts

JERUSALEM ★

OFFICIAL NAME: State of Israel
CAPITAL: Jerusalem

LAND
- Mountain Ranges: Mountains of Galilee
- Highest Peak: Mount Meron 3,963 ft. (1,208 m)
- Major River: Jordan
- Major Lakes: Dead Sea, Sea of Galilee
- Largest Desert: Negev

PEOPLE
- Population: 5,842,454 (2000 est.)
- Major Cities: Jerusalem, Tel Aviv-Jaffa, Haifa
- Official Languages: Hebrew and Arabic
- Religions: Judaism, Islam, Christianity

GOVERNMENT
- Form: Parliamentary Republic
- Chief of State: President
- Head of Government: Prime Minister
- Legislature: The Knesset
- National Anthem: "Hatikva" ("The Hope")
- Nationhood: 1948

ECONOMY
- Agriculture: Citrus and other fruits, cotton, eggs, grains, poultry, vegetables
- Manufacturing: Chemical products, electronic equipment, fertilizer, finished diamonds, paper, plastics, processed foods, scientific and optical instruments, textiles, clothing
- Mining: Potash, bromine, salt, phosphates
- Money: New Israeli shekel. (One shekel is equal to 100 agorot.)

Israel's Flag

Shekels

Timeline

late 1800s	Zionist movement begins in Europe
1947	United Nations proposes splitting Palestine into Arab and Jewish nations
1948	The State of Israel is founded; Arab nations attack Israel
1993	Israeli-PLO Peace Accord signed
2001	Peace talks between Arabs and Israelis continue

The Dead Sea

An Ancient Homeland

People have lived in Israel for thousands of years. It is the place where Abraham, the father of the Jewish people, settled with his followers. There, they built a mighty kingdom.

Israel served as a Jewish homeland for many years. Then other groups began conquering Israel. The Jewish people were forced to leave. They moved to different countries all across the world.

Meanwhile, many changes took place in Israel. Its name was changed to Palestine. Thousands of Arab people moved there. They set up their own towns and businesses.

In the late 1800s, Jewish people living in Europe started the Zionist movement. Its goal was to establish a Jewish nation in Palestine. Soon, many Jewish people began moving there. This upset the Arabs.

The Roman Empire was one of the groups that conquered Israel. In A.D. 70, they attacked Jerusalem and destroyed its Jewish temple.

David Ben-Gurion

Disagreements grew between the Jewish and Arab people living in Palestine. So in 1947, the **United Nations** proposed dividing the land into a Jewish nation and an Arab nation. Arab countries voted against the idea.

Despite disagreements, Zionist leader David Ben-Gurion proclaimed the independent State of Israel on May 14, 1948. It offered citizenship to any Jewish person willing to move to Israel.

The new Israeli nation angered the Arabs living there, as well as the neighboring Arab countries. Wars quickly began between the Israelis and the Arabs. Israel was a small, new country but it proved to be fierce. It remained in control of its land during the wars.

Today, Israel still faces problems. A group called the Palestine Liberation Organization (PLO) is trying to regain Israel's land for the Arabs. Israelis and Arabs have tried to make peace but have had little real success.

President Bill Clinton helped Israeli Prime Minister Yitzhak Rabin (L) and PLO Chairman Yasser Arafat (R) create the historic Israeli-PLO Peace Accord in 1993. Despite this, violence still continues in Israel.

The Israeli Landscape

Israel is a nation in the Middle East. Three areas in Israel are **disputed**. They are called the Golan Heights, the Gaza Strip, and the West Bank.

Western Israel borders the Mediterranean Sea. The land along the sea is a long, narrow plain. Most Israelis live there. This area contains the Plain of Esdraelon. It is a fertile area for growing crops.

Mountains rise above the land just north of the plains. The mountains of Galilee are the area's major mountain range. They contain Israel's highest point, Mount Meron.

Southern Israel is home to the Negev Desert. It makes up more than half of Israel's land. The land is very dry and hard to farm. So few people live there.

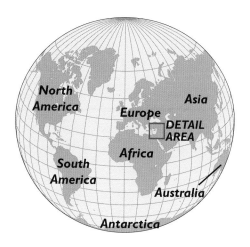

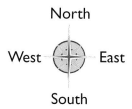

North

West — East

South

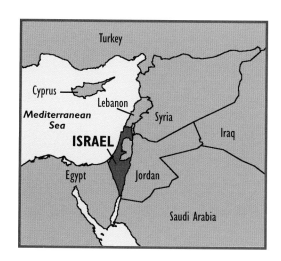

Turkey

Cyprus

Mediterranean
Sea

Lebanon

Syria

ISRAEL

Iraq

Egypt

Jordan

Saudi Arabia

Mount
Meron

**GOLAN
HEIGHTS**

CARMIEL

HAIFA

*SEA OF
GALILEE*

**MEDITERRANEAN
SEA**

PLAIN OF ESDRAELON

Jordan River

**WEST
BANK**

VALLEY

TEL AVIV-JAFFA

ASHDOD

★ **JERUSALEM**

**GAZA
STRIP**

KIRYAT GAT

DEAD SEA

**NEGEV
DESERT**

RIFT

GREAT

ELAT

Eastern Israel contains part of the Great Rift Valley. It is a long, narrow strip of land that runs along the entire length of Israel. The land has steep cliffs with low, flat land beneath.

Eastern Israel also has many important bodies of water. Northeastern Israel has a large lake called the Sea of Galilee. The Jordan River flows south from the Sea of Galilee into the Dead Sea. The Dead Sea is really a lake. It is one of the saltiest bodies of water on Earth!

The Jordan River

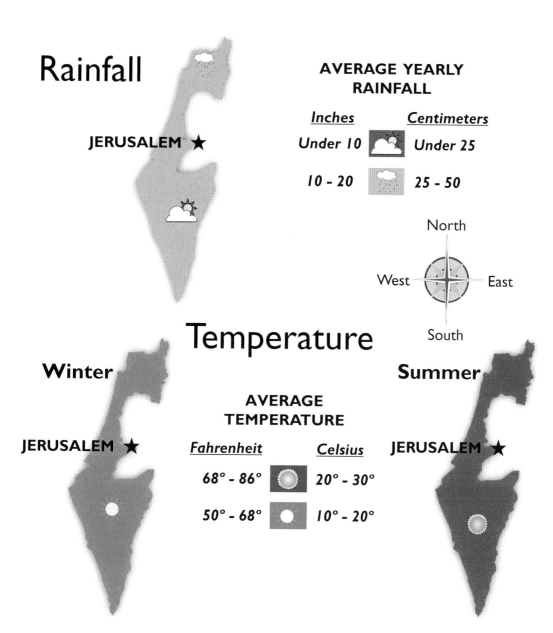

Rainfall

AVERAGE YEARLY RAINFALL

JERUSALEM ★

Inches		*Centimeters*
Under 10		Under 25
10 - 20		25 - 50

North

West ✦ East

South

Temperature

Winter

JERUSALEM ★

AVERAGE TEMPERATURE

Fahrenheit		*Celsius*
68° - 86°		20° - 30°
50° - 68°		10° - 20°

Summer

JERUSALEM ★

Plants & Animals

Northern Israel is mountainous and gets plenty of rain. This area has laurel forests and hills covered with **maquis** (ma-KEE) plants. Southern Israel is much drier. Date palms and wildflowers grow well there.

Israel is home to many animals. Large animals such as mountain gazelles, wild boars, foxes, and ibex live in Israel. Smaller animals such as gecko lizards and vipers also make their homes there. Israel is a popular stopping point for **migrating** birds.

Israel's government is working hard to protect its animals and plants. It has created about 300 national parks throughout the country.

A small sand gecko

Wildflowers blooming in the desert of Judea

The Face of Israel

Eight out of every ten Israelis are Jewish. Jewish people in Israel share a common religion, but they come from many different **ethnic** groups. Each group has its own language, food, and clothing. The blending of these groups has created a modern Israeli **culture**.

Israel is also home to many Arab people. Most are Palestinians who stayed in Israel after the country was founded in 1948. A majority of them live in northern Israel. They practice many different religions. Most are Muslim. Others are Christian or Druze.

Israel has two official languages, Hebrew and Arabic. Hebrew is the language spoken by most Jewish Israelis. Arabic is the language spoken by Arab Israelis. Some people also speak English or French. Ethnic groups throughout Israel still speak their native languages.

A Jewish family from Jerusalem

Most Israelis live in cities. Many of Israel's cities are located along the Mediterranean coast. There, people often own apartments rather than houses.

Some Israelis live in a kibbutz. It is a community where people receive food, housing, and clothing in exchange for their labor. Everyone shares the kibbutz's property. Members of a kibbutz may farm or manufacture goods.

Similar to a kibbutz is a moshav. In a moshav, each family rents its own land and owns its own home. But, the families join together to buy and sell their crops as a group.

Education is free in Israel. Children must attend school from ages 6 to 16. Jewish and Arab children attend separate schools. When they turn 18, Israeli men and women must serve in the military for two to four years.

Most Israelis wear clothing similar to that worn in the U.S. and Canada. Recent **immigrants** to Israel may still wear the traditional clothing of their homelands.

Israeli students work on homework in their school's computer lab.

The food in Israel is as varied as its people. Traditional Middle Eastern foods, such as falafel, are popular. Falafel is ground garbanzo beans that are seasoned, rolled into patties, and deep fried. Falafel is often served in flat bread with lettuce, tomatoes, and sauce.

Immigrants have also brought many new foods to Israel. Immigrants from Europe brought dishes such as chopped liver and chicken soup.

Most restaurants in Israel serve kosher foods. These foods have been prepared according to rules in the Bible. Israel also has many fast food restaurants.

A young Israeli enjoys falafel.

Hummus

Hummus is a delicious Middle Eastern food that can be eaten as a dip or sandwich spread.

2 cans garbanzo beans, drained
Juice of two small lemons
3 tbsp plain yogurt
1 tsp olive oil

1 tsp cumin
1/2 tsp coriander
1/2 tsp sugar
fresh chopped parsley

Chop garbanzo beans in a food processor. Add lemon juice, yogurt, olive oil, and spices. Mix until smooth, top with parsley, and serve.

AN IMPORTANT NOTE TO THE CHEF: Always have an adult help with the preparation and cooking of food. Never use kitchen utensils or appliances without adult permission and supervision.

English	Hebrew	Arabic
Yes	Ken	Naam
No	Lo	Laa
Thank You	Toda	Shokran
Please	Bevakasha	Min Fadlak
Hello	Shalom	Ahlan
Goodbye	Shalom	Ma as-salaamah
Mother	Ima	Omm
Father	Aba	Ab

Earning a Living

Since Israel's founding in 1948, its **economy** has grown greatly. Today, Israelis work in many different industries. People farm, manufacture goods, and work in service jobs.

Most farming in Israel is done on a kibbutz or moshav. Israel's major crops are oranges, grapefruits, cotton, peanuts, and vegetables. Israel's farmers produce enough food for the entire nation.

Many Israelis work in manufacturing jobs. They make electronic goods, build airplanes, and process foods. Diamond cutting and polishing is another major industry.

Tourism is a growing part of Israel's economy. People from all over the world visit Israel to see its ancient religious sites. This has created many service jobs. People work in restaurants, hotels, and shops.

Arab women pick carrots at a moshav in southern Israel.

City Life

Nine out of ten Israelis live in a city. Israel's cities are a blend of ancient and modern worlds.

Jerusalem is located in central Israel. It has been the historical and spiritual homeland of the Jewish people for more than 3,000 years. Today, Jerusalem serves as Israel's capital city.

Jews, Christians, and Muslims all have many holy sites in Jerusalem. Jews believe the Wailing Wall is part of an ancient Jewish temple destroyed in A.D. 70. Christians believe that many events from the **Gospel** took place in Jerusalem. Muslims believe the **prophet** Mohammed ascended to heaven in Jerusalem.

Jewish men praying at the Wailing Wall

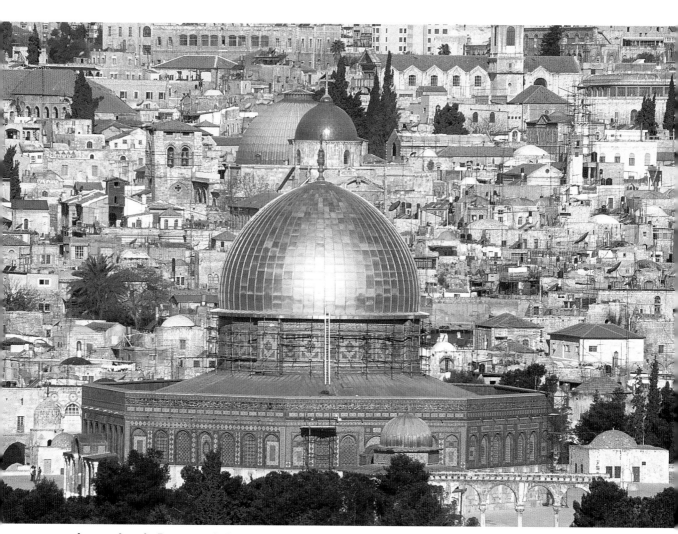

Jerusalem's Dome of the Rock is sacred to Jews and Muslims. The temple is built above a rock. Jews believe Abraham prepared to sacrifice his son there. Muslims believe it is the place where Mohammed ascended to heaven.

Another important Israeli city is Tel Aviv-Jaffa. It is located along the shores of the Mediterranean Sea. Tel Aviv was founded in 1909 as a Jewish suburb of Jaffa. After the founding of Israel, the two cities joined together.

Today, Tel Aviv-Jaffa is a bustling city. More than 300,000 people make their homes there. Many Israeli companies locate their headquarters in Tel Aviv-Jaffa. It also has wonderful beaches, museums, parks, and universities.

In the 1950s, the Israeli government began building new cities such as Carmiel and Kiryat Gat. These cities provided homes for new **immigrants** arriving to Israel. They also attracted industry to lightly populated parts of the country.

Opposite page: Tel Aviv-Jaffa

From Here to There

Israel has a good system of roads. Many people own their own cars. They either drive or take buses to get from place to place. Since Israel is such a small country, this is a quick and easy way to travel.

Israel's coastlines have several ports. Ships use the ports to carry goods in and out of Israel. Two main ports on the Mediterranean Sea are in Haifa and Ashdod. Israel also has a port in Elat, which is along the Red Sea.

A modern railway line provides another way for Israelis to travel. The railway line runs the length of the country, from north to south. It connects cities throughout Israel.

Planes fly in and out of Israel from many different countries. Israel's main airport is the David Ben-Gurion Airport in Lod. Many people fly on Israel's national airline, El Al.

Many people travel by car in Israel.

The State of Israel

Israel is a **democracy**. All citizens may vote once they turn 18. On election day, citizens cast two votes. One vote is for the prime minister. Another vote is for members of the Knesset (KENES-et).

The Knesset is Israel's lawmaking body. It has 120 members who are elected every four years. They pass Israel's laws and appoint the president.

The president's job is largely ceremonial. He or she opens the first session of the Knesset, signs treaties, and gives public speeches.

The prime minister heads Israel's government. After being elected, he or she forms a cabinet. The cabinet is Israel's main policy-making group.

Israel's Supreme Court hears the country's most serious cases. Local courts hear less serious cases. Religious courts deal with matters such as divorce.

A meeting of the Knesset

Holidays

Many of the holidays in Israel are based on the Jewish faith. Every Saturday is Shabbat. It is the weekly day of rest. People spend the day relaxing with family and friends.

Rosh Hashanah is the Jewish new year. It occurs in September. People celebrate with feasts and prayers. Eight days later, Jewish people celebrate Yom Kippur. It is a solemn day. People pray for forgiveness of their sins and fast for 25 hours.

Hanukkah celebrates how the Jews reclaimed one of their temples from the Greeks. The Jews only had enough oil to light the temple for one day. But by a miracle, the oil lasted eight days.

Purim takes place in early spring. It celebrates how Queen Esther saved the Jews from being killed by a man named Haman. On this lively holiday, children dress in costumes and get time off from school.

Passover also takes place in the spring. It marks Jewish freedom from slavery in Egypt. People celebrate by retelling the slavery story and eating a flat bread called *matza*.

Muslims in Israel celebrate Ramadan. It is a month where everyone fasts between sunrise and sunset. When the month is over, people celebrate with feasts, presents, and prayers.

Israeli children dress in costumes for Purim.

Israeli Culture

Israel's varied land makes it a great country for outdoor activities. Many people enjoy hiking at the Maktesh Ramon Crater in the Negev Desert. Swimmers and sunbathers flock to Israel's beautiful beaches.

Sports are a popular pastime in Israel. Every four years, Jewish athletes from around the world participate in the Maccabi Games. They have been held in Israel since 1932.

Music is popular in Israel. The Israel Philharmonic Orchestra is well known for its wonderful performances. Some Israeli musicians, such as violinist Itzhak Perlman, have gained fame around the world.

Israel is home to nearly 120 museums. Some museums hold ancient treasures that have been unearthed in Israel's land. Others display Israeli art. Still others honor the Jewish people killed during the **Holocaust**.

A man hikes through the Maktesh Ramon Crater.

Glossary

culture - the customs, arts, and tools of a nation or people at a certain time.

democracy - a governmental system in which the people vote on how to run the country.

dispute - an angry argument.

economy - the way a nation uses its money, goods, and natural resources.

ethnic - relating to a group of people who share a common language, culture, history, or national origin.

Gospel - the first four books in the New Testament of the Bible. They describe the life and teachings of Jesus.

Holocaust - the killing of 6 million Jews by German forces during World War II.

immigrate - to enter a country in which one was not born in order to make a permanent home there. People who do this are called immigrants.

maquis - thick, scrubby underbrush that grows along the Mediterranean shore.

migrate - to move from one place to another according to the seasons.

prophet - a religious leader who speaks as the voice of God.

United Nations - a group of nations formed in 1945. Its goals are peace, human rights, security, and social and economic development.

Web Sites

The Israeli Government's Official Web Site
http://www.israel-mfa.gov.il/mfa/home.asp
This is the Israeli government's official Web site. It has the latest Israeli news and events. This site also includes biographies of important Israeli leaders and articles on Israel's history, government, people, religions, and cultures.

The Israel Museum, Jerusalem
http://www.imj.org.il/
This site allows visitors to view items from the Israel Museum's vast collection. Visitors can wander the virtual halls of the museum, looking at Israeli art and artifacts. Or, they can participate in a virtual dig at one of Israel's many archaeological sites.

Akhlah: The Jewish Children's Learning Network
http://www.akhlah.com/
This site is aimed at young people interested in learning more about Israel and the Jewish faith. Visitors can read about Jewish holidays, learn letters and words in Hebrew, and discover Jewish heroes from the Torah.

These sites are subject to change. Go to your favorite search engine and type in "Israel" for more sites.

Index

WITHDRAWN